The Art of Troubleshooting: Strategies for Success in Engineering

Clyde Vernon

Copyright © [2023]

Title: The Art of Troubleshooting: Strategies for Success in Engineering
Author's: Clyde Vernon

All rights reserved. No part of this publication may be reproduced, stored in a retrieval system, or transmitted in any form or by any means, electronic, mechanical, photocopying, recording, or otherwise, without the prior written permission of the publisher or author, except in the case of brief quotations embodied in critical reviews and certain other non-commercial uses permitted by copyright law.

This book was printed and published by [Publisher's: **Clyde Vernon**] in [2023]

ISBN:

TABLE OF CONTENT

Chapter 1: Introduction to Troubleshooting in Engineering — 07

The Importance of Troubleshooting in Engineering

The Role of Failure Analysis in Troubleshooting

Challenges Faced in Troubleshooting

Developing a Troubleshooting Mindset

Chapter 2: Understanding the Root Causes of Failures — 15

Identifying Common Failure Modes

The Importance of Root Cause Analysis

Tools and Techniques for Identifying Root Causes

Chapter 3: Problem Solving Strategies for Troubleshooting 21

The Scientific Method in Troubleshooting

Developing Hypotheses and Testing Them

Data Collection and Analysis in Troubleshooting

Decision Making in Troubleshooting

Chapter 4: Communication and Collaboration in Troubleshooting 29

Effective Communication Skills for Troubleshooters

Collaborative Problem Solving Techniques

Building Cross-Functional Teams for Troubleshooting

Chapter 5: Tools and Techniques for Troubleshooting 35

Diagnostic Tools and Equipment

Statistical Process Control for Troubleshooting

Failure Mode and Effects Analysis (FMEA)

Design of Experiments (DOE) in Troubleshooting

Chapter 6: Case Studies in Troubleshooting   44

Case Study 1: Mechanical Failure in a Manufacturing Plant

Case Study 2: Electrical System Malfunction in a Power Plant

Case Study 3: Software Bug in a Computer System

Chapter 7: Preventive Measures and Continuous Improvement   51

Implementing Proactive Maintenance Strategies

Lessons Learned from Failure Analysis

Continuous Improvement in Troubleshooting Processes

Chapter 8: Troubleshooting in Specific Engineering Disciplines   57

Mechanical Engineering Troubleshooting Strategies

Electrical Engineering Troubleshooting Strategies

Civil Engineering Troubleshooting Strategies

Software Engineering Troubleshooting Strategies

Chapter 9: Troubleshooting Challenges in Emerging Technologies 66

Troubleshooting in Renewable Energy Systems

Troubleshooting in Internet of Things (IoT) Devices

Troubleshooting in Artificial Intelligence Systems

Chapter 10: Professional Development for Troubleshooters 73

Continuous Learning in Troubleshooting

Certifications and Training for Troubleshooters

Networking and Knowledge Sharing Opportunities

Chapter 11: Conclusion and Final Thoughts 79

Recap of Key Strategies for Successful Troubleshooting

The Future of Troubleshooting in Engineering

Chapter 1: Introduction to Troubleshooting in Engineering

The Importance of Troubleshooting in Engineering

In the world of engineering, troubleshooting plays a vital role in ensuring the success and efficiency of any project. It is a problem-solving technique that involves identifying, analyzing, and resolving issues that may arise during the development, production, or maintenance of a product or system. Troubleshooting is an essential skill for every engineer, particularly those in the field of manufacturing engineering, where complex machinery and processes are involved.

One of the primary reasons why troubleshooting holds such significance in engineering is its ability to minimize downtime. In manufacturing engineering, any disruption in the production process can result in significant financial losses. By employing effective troubleshooting strategies, engineers can quickly identify the root cause of a problem and implement appropriate solutions, thereby minimizing downtime and ensuring smooth operations.

Moreover, troubleshooting also contributes to the overall quality and reliability of the final product. Through a systematic approach, engineers can identify and rectify any design flaws or performance issues, ensuring that the product meets the required specifications and standards. This not only enhances customer satisfaction but also improves the reputation of the company in the market.

Furthermore, troubleshooting fosters innovation and continuous improvement in the field of engineering. By analyzing and understanding the causes of problems, engineers can develop innovative solutions that not only resolve the immediate issue but also prevent similar problems from occurring in the future. This continual learning and improvement are essential for staying competitive in the ever-evolving manufacturing engineering industry.

In addition to technical skills, troubleshooting also requires strong analytical and problem-solving abilities. Engineers must be able to think critically and logically, dissecting complex systems to identify the underlying problems. Effective troubleshooting also involves effective communication and collaboration, as engineers often need to work in teams to resolve issues collectively.

In conclusion, the importance of troubleshooting in engineering, particularly in the field of manufacturing engineering, cannot be overstated. It is a skill that enables engineers to minimize downtime, improve product quality, foster innovation, and continuously improve processes. By honing their troubleshooting skills, engineers can ensure the success and efficiency of their projects, ultimately contributing to the growth and development of the manufacturing industry as a whole.

The Role of Failure Analysis in Troubleshooting

In the field of manufacturing engineering, troubleshooting is an essential skill that ensures smooth operations and minimizes downtime. When a problem arises in a manufacturing process, it is crucial to identify and rectify the root cause swiftly to prevent further complications. Failure analysis plays a critical role in this process, as it allows engineers to understand the underlying reasons behind failures and develop effective solutions.

Failure analysis is a systematic approach that involves investigating and examining failed components or systems to determine the cause of failure. It utilizes various techniques such as visual inspection, material analysis, and testing to gather data and evidence. By analyzing the failed components, engineers can gain valuable insights into the design, manufacturing, or operational issues contributing to the failure.

One of the primary benefits of failure analysis is its ability to prevent recurring failures. By identifying the root cause, engineers can implement corrective measures that eliminate the problem permanently. This not only saves time and resources but also improves the overall reliability and quality of the manufacturing process.

Additionally, failure analysis helps in identifying potential safety hazards. Understanding the causes of failure can reveal weaknesses in the system that may pose risks to workers or the environment. By addressing these issues promptly, manufacturers can create a safer working environment and adhere to regulatory standards.

Moreover, failure analysis can aid in product improvement and innovation. By studying failed components, engineers can identify areas for design or material enhancements. This knowledge can be used to develop more robust and durable products, leading to improved customer satisfaction and market competitiveness.

Another aspect to consider is the financial impact of failure analysis. Downtime caused by equipment failures can result in significant financial losses for manufacturers. By conducting a thorough failure analysis, engineers can reduce downtime by quickly identifying the root cause and implementing the appropriate solutions. This proactive approach not only saves money but also increases productivity and customer satisfaction.

In conclusion, failure analysis plays a vital role in troubleshooting for manufacturing engineering professionals. It allows engineers to understand the underlying causes of failures, prevent recurring issues, improve product quality, ensure safety, and reduce financial losses. By utilizing failure analysis techniques effectively, engineers can troubleshoot with confidence and ensure the smooth functioning of manufacturing processes.

Challenges Faced in Troubleshooting

Troubleshooting is an essential skill in the field of manufacturing engineering. It involves identifying and resolving issues that arise during the production process. However, this task is not without its challenges. In this subchapter, we will explore some of the common challenges faced in troubleshooting and provide strategies for success.

One of the primary challenges in troubleshooting is the complexity of modern manufacturing systems. These systems often consist of numerous interconnected components, making it difficult to pinpoint the exact source of a problem. This complexity can lead to a time-consuming and frustrating process of elimination. To overcome this challenge, engineers must have a deep understanding of the system's design and functionality. They should also possess strong analytical skills and the ability to break down complex problems into smaller, more manageable parts.

Another challenge is the constant evolution of technology in the manufacturing industry. As new technologies are introduced, engineers must continuously update their knowledge and skills to keep up. This can be particularly challenging for experienced professionals who may be more accustomed to traditional methods. To address this challenge, it is crucial to invest in ongoing training and professional development. Staying up-to-date with the latest technological advancements will not only enhance troubleshooting abilities but also improve overall efficiency and productivity.

Time constraints are also a significant challenge in troubleshooting. In a manufacturing setting, every minute of downtime can result in substantial financial losses. Therefore, engineers must be able to quickly identify and resolve issues to minimize the impact on production. This requires a combination of experience, intuition, and efficient problem-solving techniques. It is essential to prioritize tasks, focus on the most critical problems, and utilize available resources effectively.

Communication is yet another challenge in troubleshooting, especially in large manufacturing facilities where multiple teams and departments are involved. Clear and effective communication is crucial for sharing information, coordinating efforts, and ensuring everyone is on the same page. Additionally, engineers may need to communicate complex technical concepts to non-technical stakeholders. Developing excellent communication skills, both written and verbal, is essential for successful troubleshooting.

In conclusion, troubleshooting in manufacturing engineering can be a complex and challenging task. The complexity of modern systems, rapid technological advancements, time constraints, and communication issues are some of the challenges engineers face. However, with the right strategies, including a deep understanding of the systems, ongoing training, efficient problem-solving techniques, and excellent communication skills, these challenges can be overcome. By mastering the art of troubleshooting, engineers can ensure smooth production processes, minimize downtime, and contribute to the success of manufacturing operations.

Developing a Troubleshooting Mindset

In the world of manufacturing engineering, troubleshooting is an essential skill that can make or break the success of a project. Whether you are a seasoned engineer or just starting out in the field, developing a troubleshooting mindset is crucial for overcoming challenges and achieving success.

The first step in developing a troubleshooting mindset is to embrace a curious and inquisitive nature. Instead of viewing problems as roadblocks, see them as opportunities for growth and learning. Ask questions, dig deeper, and challenge assumptions. This mindset allows you to approach problems with an open mind and find creative solutions.

Another important aspect of developing a troubleshooting mindset is to cultivate patience and persistence. Problem-solving can be a time-consuming process, requiring you to analyze data, conduct experiments, and explore different possibilities. It is easy to get frustrated and give up when facing complex issues, but remember that perseverance is key. Break down the problem into smaller, manageable tasks and celebrate small victories along the way.

A troubleshooting mindset also involves developing strong analytical skills. This includes the ability to gather and analyze data, identify patterns, and make informed decisions. Take advantage of tools and resources available to you, such as statistical analysis software or data visualization tools. By leveraging these resources, you can make more accurate assessments and develop effective solutions.

Furthermore, developing a troubleshooting mindset requires effective communication and collaboration skills. Engage with colleagues, share your insights, and seek input from others. Two heads are often better than one, and collaborating with others can lead to innovative solutions that you may not have thought of on your own.

Finally, it is important to embrace a continuous improvement mindset. Troubleshooting is not a one-time event, but an ongoing process. Learn from past experiences, document lessons learned, and continuously seek ways to refine your troubleshooting skills. By constantly striving for improvement, you will not only become a more effective troubleshooter but also contribute to the overall success of your organization.

In conclusion, developing a troubleshooting mindset is essential for success in manufacturing engineering. Embrace curiosity, be patient and persistent, hone your analytical skills, collaborate with others, and embrace a continuous improvement mindset. By adopting these strategies, you will be well-equipped to overcome challenges, find innovative solutions, and thrive in the field of manufacturing engineering.

Chapter 2: Understanding the Root Causes of Failures

Identifying Common Failure Modes

In the field of manufacturing engineering, understanding the common failure modes is crucial for troubleshooting and ensuring the success of any project. By recognizing these failure modes, engineers can take proactive measures to prevent and mitigate them, ultimately leading to improved efficiency and productivity.

One of the most common failure modes in manufacturing engineering is equipment malfunction. Machines and tools can break down due to wear and tear, inadequate maintenance, or faulty components. Identifying the root cause of equipment malfunction is essential to minimize downtime and prevent costly repairs. Regular inspections, preventive maintenance, and monitoring equipment performance are effective strategies to identify and address potential issues before they escalate.

Another common failure mode is human error. Manufacturing processes often involve various tasks that require manual intervention. Errors can occur at any stage, from design and planning to execution and quality control. Recognizing the potential for human error and implementing measures such as standardized operating procedures, training programs, and error-proofing techniques can greatly reduce the occurrence of mistakes and ensure consistent quality.

Material failure is another significant failure mode in manufacturing engineering. Whether it's the use of wrong materials, poor material handling, or inadequate quality control, material failure can lead to product defects and safety hazards. Thorough material testing, supplier audits, and strict quality control measures can help identify and prevent material-related issues.

Inadequate process design and optimization can also result in failure modes. Poorly designed workflows, inefficient layouts, and inadequate process controls can lead to bottlenecks, delays, and suboptimal productivity. Conducting process audits, utilizing lean manufacturing principles, and continuously monitoring and refining processes can help identify and rectify shortcomings, improving overall efficiency and reducing waste.

Furthermore, environmental factors and external influences can contribute to failure modes in manufacturing engineering. Temperature variations, humidity, power fluctuations, and other external factors may impact the performance and reliability of equipment and processes. Recognizing these factors and implementing appropriate measures such as climate control systems, backup power solutions, and robust contingency plans can minimize the impact of external influences on manufacturing operations.

In conclusion, identifying common failure modes is essential for manufacturing engineering professionals to troubleshoot effectively and ensure successful outcomes. By proactively addressing equipment malfunction, human errors, material failures, process design flaws, and environmental factors, engineers can optimize manufacturing processes, improve productivity, and enhance product quality. Through continuous monitoring, analysis, and improvement, manufacturing engineering professionals can minimize failure modes and contribute to the success of their projects.

The Importance of Root Cause Analysis

In the field of manufacturing engineering, troubleshooting is an essential skill that determines the success of any project. When issues arise, it is crucial to identify the root cause rather than focusing solely on resolving the immediate problem. This is where Root Cause Analysis (RCA) comes into play, a systematic approach that helps engineers identify the underlying causes of issues and develop effective solutions.

RCA is a problem-solving technique that goes beyond fixing symptoms and delves deep into the core of the problem. By understanding the root cause, engineers can prevent future occurrences and improve overall efficiency. This subchapter will explore the importance of RCA in manufacturing engineering and how it can benefit professionals in this field.

One of the main advantages of RCA is its ability to prevent recurring issues. By identifying the root cause, engineers can implement targeted solutions that eliminate the problem at its source. This saves time, resources, and prevents production delays, ultimately leading to increased productivity and customer satisfaction.

Furthermore, RCA helps engineers gain a comprehensive understanding of the manufacturing process. It allows them to analyze data, identify patterns, and make informed decisions based on evidence. By leveraging this knowledge, engineers can optimize processes, reduce waste, and enhance quality control measures.

In addition to preventing future issues and improving efficiency, RCA also fosters a culture of continuous improvement within the manufacturing engineering field. By encouraging engineers to explore the root cause of problems, organizations create an environment that values innovation and learning. This empowers individuals to think critically, adapt to new challenges, and develop creative solutions.

Moreover, RCA promotes collaboration and teamwork. When engineers work together to analyze problems, they share knowledge and perspectives, leading to more comprehensive solutions. This enhances communication within the team, boosts morale, and promotes a sense of ownership and accountability.

In conclusion, Root Cause Analysis is a vital aspect of troubleshooting in the field of manufacturing engineering. By focusing on the underlying causes rather than superficial symptoms, engineers can develop effective solutions that prevent recurring issues, improve efficiency, and foster a culture of continuous improvement. Embracing RCA as a problem-solving technique empowers professionals in manufacturing engineering to overcome challenges and drive success in their projects.

Tools and Techniques for Identifying Root Causes

When it comes to troubleshooting problems in the field of manufacturing engineering, identifying the root cause is essential for finding effective solutions. Without a clear understanding of what is causing the issue, it is nearly impossible to implement fixes that will prevent its recurrence. This subchapter delves into the various tools and techniques that can be utilized to identify the underlying causes of problems in manufacturing engineering.

One of the primary tools used in this process is the cause-and-effect diagram, also known as the Ishikawa or fishbone diagram. This graphical representation allows engineers to visually map out all possible causes contributing to a specific problem. By categorizing potential causes into different branches, such as people, methods, machines, materials, and environment, the cause-and-effect diagram helps guide the investigation towards a comprehensive analysis.

Another valuable technique for identifying root causes is the 5 Whys method. By repeatedly asking "why" in response to each answer, this technique helps to uncover deeper layers of causality. It encourages individuals to think critically and dig beyond the surface-level symptoms. By consistently asking "why" at least five times, engineers can trace the problem back to its root cause, leading to a more robust solution.

Data analysis is also crucial in troubleshooting manufacturing engineering issues. Statistical tools, such as Pareto charts, can help identify the most significant contributing factors. These charts prioritize the causes by their frequency of occurrence, allowing engineers to focus their efforts on the most influential factors. Additionally, trend analysis and control charts can provide insights into patterns and variations in data, enabling engineers to pinpoint anomalies and root causes.

In some cases, physical inspection and testing may be necessary to identify root causes. Non-destructive testing techniques, like X-ray, ultrasonic testing, and thermography, can reveal hidden defects or abnormalities in materials or structures. These techniques aid in the identification of root causes that are not apparent through visual inspection alone.

Lastly, collaboration and brainstorming sessions with cross-functional teams can be beneficial in identifying root causes. Different perspectives and expertise from various departments or individuals can help uncover potential causes that may have been overlooked. By collectively analyzing the problem, engineers can gain a holistic understanding of the situation and identify the most probable root causes.

In conclusion, the tools and techniques for identifying root causes discussed in this subchapter provide valuable strategies for effective troubleshooting in manufacturing engineering. From cause-and-effect diagrams to statistical analysis and physical inspections, each method plays a vital role in the identification of underlying issues. By employing these tools and techniques, engineers can enhance their problem-solving capabilities and contribute to more efficient and successful manufacturing processes.

Chapter 3: Problem Solving Strategies for Troubleshooting

The Scientific Method in Troubleshooting

In the field of manufacturing engineering, troubleshooting is an essential skill that allows professionals to identify and resolve problems efficiently. However, troubleshooting is not just a matter of guesswork or trial and error. It requires a systematic and analytical approach, which is where the scientific method comes into play.

The scientific method is a well-established framework that scientists use to investigate and understand natural phenomena. It involves a series of steps that guide researchers in formulating hypotheses, testing them, and drawing conclusions. This same method can be applied to troubleshooting in manufacturing engineering to increase the chances of finding effective solutions.

The first step of the scientific method in troubleshooting is to clearly define the problem. This involves understanding the symptoms, gathering relevant data, and interviewing those who have observed or experienced the issue. By gathering as much information as possible, engineers can form a hypothesis about the root cause of the problem.

The next step is to design and conduct experiments to test the hypothesis. This may involve manipulating variables, collecting data, and analyzing the results. In troubleshooting, experiments can take the form of simulations, physical tests, or even virtual models. The goal is to gather evidence that either supports or refutes the initial hypothesis.

Once the experiments are complete, the data must be analyzed and interpreted. This step requires a keen eye for patterns, correlations, and trends. Engineers must be able to draw meaningful conclusions from the data and use them to refine their understanding of the problem.

Based on the analysis, engineers can then develop and implement a solution. This may involve making changes to processes, equipment, or materials. It is crucial to document the solution and its implementation to ensure its effectiveness and to share the knowledge with others in the field.

Finally, the scientific method emphasizes the importance of evaluation and reflection. Engineers should assess the effectiveness of the implemented solution and consider any unintended consequences or further improvements that may be necessary.

By applying the scientific method to troubleshooting in manufacturing engineering, professionals can approach problems in a logical and systematic manner. This method helps to eliminate guesswork and increases the chances of finding long-lasting and effective solutions. Ultimately, the scientific method in troubleshooting allows engineers to optimize processes, increase productivity, and ensure the smooth functioning of manufacturing systems.

Developing Hypotheses and Testing Them

In the realm of manufacturing engineering, troubleshooting is an essential skill. It requires a systematic approach to identify and solve problems efficiently. One of the key elements of successful troubleshooting is the development and testing of hypotheses. This subchapter will delve into this critical aspect of troubleshooting, providing valuable insights and strategies for success in engineering.

When faced with a problem, it is crucial to gather relevant information and analyze the available data. This data analysis will help you formulate hypotheses, which are educated guesses about the potential causes of the problem. Developing hypotheses is a creative process that involves drawing upon your knowledge, experience, and intuition.

To effectively develop hypotheses, it is imperative to consider all possible causes of the problem. This requires a comprehensive understanding of the system, its components, and their interactions. By systematically evaluating the information at hand, you can generate multiple hypotheses, each addressing a different potential cause.

Once you have developed your hypotheses, it is time to put them to the test. Testing hypotheses involves designing and conducting experiments or investigations to gather additional data and evidence. This helps you validate or refute your hypotheses, leading you closer to identifying the root cause of the problem.

In the testing phase, it is crucial to maintain objectivity and rigor. You must ensure that your experiments are well-designed, with controlled variables and reliable measurements. By following a systematic approach, you can eliminate biases and obtain accurate results.

It is important to note that testing hypotheses is an iterative process. As you gather more data and evidence, you may need to refine or modify your hypotheses. This continuous refinement allows you to narrow down the potential causes until you reach a definitive conclusion.

Developing hypotheses and testing them requires a combination of technical knowledge, critical thinking skills, and creativity. It is a fundamental aspect of troubleshooting in manufacturing engineering, enabling engineers to identify and resolve complex problems efficiently.

In conclusion, the ability to develop hypotheses and test them is a vital skill for manufacturing engineers. By employing a systematic approach and leveraging available data, engineers can generate educated guesses about the causes of a problem. Testing these hypotheses through well-designed experiments allows for the validation or refutation of potential causes, leading to the identification of the root cause. This subchapter has provided valuable insights and strategies for successfully developing and testing hypotheses, enabling engineers to excel in troubleshooting and problem-solving.

Data Collection and Analysis in Troubleshooting

In the field of manufacturing engineering, troubleshooting plays a crucial role in identifying and resolving issues that may arise during the production process. To effectively troubleshoot, engineers need to rely on accurate data collection and analysis techniques. This subchapter will delve into the importance of data collection and analysis in troubleshooting and provide valuable strategies for success in the manufacturing engineering niche.

Data collection serves as the foundation of effective troubleshooting. By gathering relevant data, engineers can gain a comprehensive understanding of the problem at hand. This includes gathering information about the equipment, processes, and variables involved in the manufacturing process. Collecting data from multiple sources, such as sensors, quality control systems, and operator feedback, allows engineers to obtain a holistic view of the situation.

Once data is collected, the next step is analysis. Analysis involves organizing, interpreting, and drawing conclusions from the data. Various analytical techniques can be employed, including statistical analysis, trend analysis, and root cause analysis. Through these techniques, engineers can identify patterns, anomalies, and potential causes of the problem. This analysis provides a solid basis for designing effective troubleshooting strategies.

In troubleshooting, data collection and analysis go hand in hand. Accurate data collection ensures that the analysis is based on reliable information, while effective analysis provides insights that guide further data collection. The iterative nature of this process helps engineers to refine their understanding of the problem and develop more targeted solutions.

To excel in data collection and analysis, engineers should employ a systematic approach. This includes clearly defining the problem, identifying the required data, and selecting appropriate data collection methods. Engineers should also be proficient in data analysis techniques, such as using statistical software and visualization tools.

Moreover, engineers should be aware of potential challenges in data collection and analysis. These challenges include data accuracy, data consistency, and data integrity. By addressing these challenges and employing best practices, engineers can ensure that their troubleshooting efforts are based on reliable and relevant data.

In conclusion, data collection and analysis are fundamental components of troubleshooting in manufacturing engineering. By employing systematic approaches and utilizing various analytical techniques, engineers can effectively identify and resolve issues in the production process. Building expertise in data collection and analysis is essential for success in troubleshooting, enabling engineers to optimize manufacturing processes and achieve greater efficiency and quality.

Decision Making in Troubleshooting

In the field of manufacturing engineering, troubleshooting is an essential skill that every professional must possess. It is the process of identifying and resolving problems that arise in the production line, ensuring smooth and efficient operations. However, effective troubleshooting requires not only technical expertise but also sound decision-making skills. This subchapter aims to explore the art of decision making in troubleshooting, providing valuable strategies for success in engineering.

When faced with a problem in manufacturing, the first step in decision-making is to gather information. This involves understanding the symptoms, observing the production line, and collecting relevant data. By analyzing the available information, engineers can identify the root cause of the issue and develop potential solutions.

Once the information is gathered, engineers need to evaluate the available options. This requires considering the feasibility, cost-effectiveness, and potential impact of each solution. It is crucial to involve stakeholders, such as operators and managers, in the decision-making process to ensure a comprehensive understanding of the problem and its implications.

Furthermore, effective decision making in troubleshooting requires a systematic approach. Engineers should create a framework for evaluating and prioritizing potential solutions based on their feasibility, probability of success, and potential risks. This allows for a structured decision-making process, minimizing the chances of overlooking crucial factors.

In some cases, engineers may encounter complex problems that require a more collaborative approach. Decision-making in troubleshooting can benefit from the expertise of cross-functional teams, where individuals from different departments collaborate to find the best solution. This diversity of perspectives can lead to more innovative and effective problem-solving.

Additionally, it is important for engineers to consider the long-term implications of their decisions. Troubleshooting is not just about fixing immediate problems but also about preventing their recurrence. By addressing underlying causes and implementing preventive measures, engineers can ensure long-term success in troubleshooting.

In conclusion, decision making is a critical aspect of troubleshooting in manufacturing engineering. By gathering information, evaluating options, following a systematic approach, and considering long-term implications, engineers can make informed decisions that lead to effective problem resolution. Moreover, involving stakeholders and utilizing cross-functional teams can enhance the decision-making process by incorporating diverse perspectives. Ultimately, mastering the art of decision making in troubleshooting is essential for success in the field of manufacturing engineering.

Chapter 4: Communication and Collaboration in Troubleshooting

Effective Communication Skills for Troubleshooters

In the fast-paced field of manufacturing engineering, the ability to effectively communicate is crucial for troubleshooters. Whether you are identifying and resolving problems on the production line or working on complex machinery, having strong communication skills can make all the difference in finding successful solutions. This subchapter will explore the essential communication skills that every troubleshooter in the manufacturing engineering niche should possess.

First and foremost, active listening is a fundamental skill that must be honed. Troubleshooters must listen attentively to the concerns and descriptions of problems shared by operators, engineers, and other team members. By actively listening, troubleshooters can obtain all the relevant details needed to tackle the issue effectively. Additionally, this skill allows troubleshooters to empathize with the frustrations and challenges faced by their colleagues, fostering a sense of teamwork and collaboration.

Clear and concise communication is equally important. Troubleshooters must be able to articulate their thoughts and ideas in a manner that is easily understood by others. This includes using simple and straightforward language, avoiding technical jargon whenever possible. By communicating clearly, troubleshooters can ensure that their recommendations and instructions are effectively conveyed, minimizing the risk of miscommunication and potential errors.

Furthermore, troubleshooters should develop strong interpersonal skills to foster positive relationships within the team. This involves being approachable, respectful, and maintaining a proactive attitude towards problem-solving. Building trust and rapport with colleagues can be invaluable in troubleshooting situations, as it encourages open and honest communication, leading to more accurate problem identification and innovative solutions.

In addition to verbal communication skills, written communication skills are also essential for troubleshooters. Clear and concise documentation of troubleshooting processes, steps, and findings can greatly assist in future problem-solving endeavors. This documentation creates a valuable resource that can be referred to by others, ensuring continuity and efficiency in resolving similar issues that may arise in the future.

In conclusion, effective communication skills are vital for troubleshooters in the manufacturing engineering niche. Active listening, clear and concise communication, strong interpersonal skills, and effective written communication all contribute to successful troubleshooting. By developing and honing these skills, troubleshooters can enhance their ability to identify, analyze, and resolve problems efficiently, thus ensuring the smooth operation of manufacturing processes and contributing to the overall success of the organization.

Collaborative Problem Solving Techniques

In the field of manufacturing engineering, problem-solving skills are crucial for success. As engineers, we are constantly faced with various challenges that require innovative solutions. However, more often than not, these problems are complex and cannot be tackled by an individual alone. This is where collaborative problem-solving techniques come into play.

Collaborative problem solving involves bringing together individuals with diverse expertise and perspectives to collectively address a problem. By leveraging the skills and knowledge of a team, the chances of finding an effective solution are significantly increased. This subchapter will delve into some key techniques that can enhance collaborative problem-solving in the manufacturing engineering domain.

1. Brainstorming: This technique involves gathering a group of individuals and encouraging them to generate as many ideas as possible. The emphasis is on quantity rather than quality at this stage. By creating a safe and non-judgmental environment, team members can freely express their ideas, which can then be refined and combined to form innovative solutions.

2. Root Cause Analysis: Often, manufacturing engineering problems are just symptoms of underlying issues. Conducting a root cause analysis helps identify the fundamental cause of the problem, enabling the team to address it at its source. This technique involves asking 'why' multiple times to uncover the deeper reasons behind the problem.

3. Fishbone Diagrams: Also known as Ishikawa diagrams, these visual tools help identify potential causes of a problem. By categorizing causes into different branches, the team can systematically analyze and prioritize each potential cause. This technique aids in understanding the interdependencies between various factors and guides the team towards effective problem-solving.

4. Failure Mode and Effects Analysis (FMEA): FMEA is a proactive approach to problem-solving that focuses on identifying and mitigating potential failures before they occur. By systematically assessing the risks associated with each failure mode, the team can prioritize actions and allocate resources accordingly.

5. Six Thinking Hats: This technique, developed by Edward de Bono, involves assigning different roles to team members during problem-solving discussions. Each role represents a different perspective, such as critical thinking, creativity, or emotional analysis. By wearing different "hats," team members can approach the problem from various angles, facilitating a more comprehensive analysis.

Collaborative problem-solving techniques empower manufacturing engineering teams to tackle complex problems more effectively. By leveraging the expertise and perspectives of individuals, these techniques foster creativity and innovation, leading to optimal solutions. By implementing these techniques, engineers can enhance their troubleshooting skills and achieve success in their endeavors. Remember, effective problem-solving is a team effort, and together, we can overcome any challenge.

Building Cross-Functional Teams for Troubleshooting

In today's complex and ever-evolving world of manufacturing engineering, troubleshooting is an essential skill that ensures smooth operations and avoids costly downtime. However, effective troubleshooting often requires more than just technical expertise. It necessitates the collaboration of cross-functional teams that bring together individuals with diverse skills and perspectives. This subchapter aims to provide valuable insights into building and managing such teams for successful troubleshooting in the manufacturing engineering industry.

The key to building cross-functional teams is to assemble individuals with complementary skills and knowledge. Each team member should possess a unique expertise or specialization that contributes to the overall problem-solving process. By incorporating individuals from different departments, such as operations, maintenance, quality control, and production, the team can leverage a wide range of perspectives to identify and address issues more effectively.

To foster collaboration within the team, it is crucial to establish a culture of open communication and mutual respect. Encourage team members to share their ideas, suggestions, and concerns freely, creating an environment where everyone feels valued and heard. This open dialogue allows for the exploration of diverse perspectives and the generation of innovative solutions.

Additionally, effective team leaders play a vital role in managing cross-functional teams. A skilled leader understands the strengths and weaknesses of each team member and allocates tasks accordingly.

They encourage teamwork, facilitate effective communication, and ensure that everyone is aligned towards a common goal. Furthermore, leaders must establish clear roles and responsibilities, ensuring that each team member understands their contribution to the troubleshooting process.

Regular team meetings are essential for maintaining momentum and tracking progress. These meetings provide an opportunity to discuss ongoing issues, share updates, and brainstorm potential solutions. It is crucial to establish a structured approach to problem-solving, utilizing tools such as root cause analysis, fishbone diagrams, or the 5 Whys technique. These methodologies help the team dig deep into the problem's underlying causes, facilitating effective troubleshooting.

In conclusion, building cross-functional teams for troubleshooting in the manufacturing engineering industry is essential for success. By assembling individuals with diverse skills and perspectives, fostering open communication, and providing effective leadership, these teams can tackle complex issues more efficiently. Through a structured problem-solving approach and regular collaboration, cross-functional teams can drive continuous improvement and ensure the smooth functioning of manufacturing processes.

Chapter 5: Tools and Techniques for Troubleshooting

Diagnostic Tools and Equipment

In the field of manufacturing engineering, troubleshooting and problem-solving skills are essential for success. As a manufacturing engineer, it is crucial to be able to identify and resolve issues quickly and efficiently to ensure the smooth operation of production processes. This subchapter will explore the various diagnostic tools and equipment that can aid in troubleshooting, allowing engineers to pinpoint problems accurately and implement effective solutions.

One of the most common diagnostic tools used in manufacturing engineering is the multimeter. This versatile device can measure electrical voltage, current, and resistance, helping engineers identify electrical faults in machinery and equipment. By using a multimeter, manufacturing engineers can quickly identify faulty connections, damaged components, or power supply issues, enabling them to take corrective measures promptly.

Another valuable diagnostic tool is the oscilloscope. This device is used to measure and analyze electronic signals, allowing engineers to visualize waveforms and identify irregularities or anomalies. By observing the signals produced by different components within a system, manufacturing engineers can diagnose faulty parts and troubleshoot electronic circuits effectively.

In addition to electrical diagnostic tools, mechanical diagnostic equipment is also crucial in manufacturing engineering. Vibration analyzers, for example, are used to measure and analyze vibrations in machinery. Excessive vibrations can indicate misalignments, loose components, or worn-out bearings, which can lead to equipment failure or reduced performance. By using vibration analyzers, manufacturing engineers can detect and resolve these issues before they escalate.

Thermal imaging cameras are another valuable tool for manufacturing engineers. These cameras use infrared technology to detect variations in temperature, allowing engineers to identify overheating components or faulty insulation. By pinpointing areas of high temperature, manufacturing engineers can prevent equipment damage, optimize performance, and ensure worker safety.

Lastly, computer diagnostic software plays a crucial role in troubleshooting complex systems. These software programs can analyze data, detect abnormalities, and provide insights into potential issues. By utilizing computer diagnostic tools, manufacturing engineers can streamline the troubleshooting process and improve the accuracy of their diagnoses.

In conclusion, diagnostic tools and equipment are essential for manufacturing engineers to effectively troubleshoot and resolve issues in their field. From multimeters and oscilloscopes to vibration analyzers and thermal imaging cameras, these tools enable engineers to identify problems accurately and implement timely solutions. Additionally, computer diagnostic software aids in analyzing complex systems, streamlining the troubleshooting process. By utilizing these diagnostic tools and equipment, manufacturing engineers can ensure the smooth operation of production processes, minimize downtime, and ultimately contribute to the success of the manufacturing industry.

Statistical Process Control for Troubleshooting

In the world of manufacturing engineering, troubleshooting is an essential skill that ensures the smooth operation of production processes and the delivery of high-quality products. One powerful tool that can aid in troubleshooting is Statistical Process Control (SPC). SPC allows engineers to monitor and control the variability of a process, enabling them to identify and address issues before they become major problems.

SPC involves the use of statistical techniques to measure and analyze process data. By collecting data over time, engineers can identify trends, patterns, and abnormalities that may indicate a problem within the process. This data-driven approach provides valuable insights into the root causes of issues, allowing engineers to make informed decisions and take appropriate corrective actions.

One of the key benefits of SPC is its ability to differentiate between common cause variation and special cause variation. Common cause variation refers to the inherent variability present in any process, while special cause variation is caused by specific factors that are not part of the normal process. By understanding the different types of variation, engineers can focus their troubleshooting efforts on addressing special causes, which have a greater impact on process performance.

To implement SPC effectively, engineers need to establish control charts, which are graphical representations of process data over time. Control charts display the process mean and control limits, which help engineers identify when the process is operating within acceptable limits or when it is exhibiting abnormal behavior. When a data point falls outside the control limits or shows a significant trend, it signals the presence of a special cause variation that requires investigation and intervention.

SPC also enables engineers to establish process capability indices, which measure the ability of a process to meet specified requirements. These indices provide a quantitative assessment of process performance and can help identify areas for improvement. By continuously monitoring process capability, engineers can proactively address potential issues and optimize the manufacturing process.

In summary, Statistical Process Control is a valuable tool for troubleshooting in manufacturing engineering. By using statistical techniques to monitor and analyze process data, engineers can identify and address issues before they escalate into major problems. SPC allows for the differentiation between common cause and special cause variation, enabling engineers to focus their efforts on addressing specific factors that impact process performance. With the use of control charts and process capability indices, engineers can effectively monitor and improve the manufacturing process, ensuring high-quality products and efficient operations.

Failure Mode and Effects Analysis (FMEA)

In the field of engineering, troubleshooting plays a crucial role in identifying and resolving problems to ensure smooth operation and maximum efficiency. One powerful tool that helps engineers tackle potential failures is Failure Mode and Effects Analysis (FMEA). FMEA is a systematic approach that allows engineers to proactively identify possible failure modes and their potential effects on a manufacturing process.

Manufacturing engineering, in particular, heavily relies on FMEA to improve product quality, reduce costs, and enhance overall performance. This subchapter aims to provide a comprehensive understanding of FMEA and its application in the manufacturing engineering niche.

To begin, FMEA involves a step-by-step evaluation of a system, product, or process to identify potential failure modes and their effects. By analyzing failure modes and their associated effects, engineers can develop strategies to prevent or mitigate failures before they occur. FMEA also helps in prioritizing risks and allocating resources effectively.

One of the key benefits of FMEA is its ability to enhance product reliability. By identifying potential failure modes early in the design or manufacturing process, engineers can make necessary modifications to prevent failures. This proactive approach saves time and costs associated with rework, recalls, or customer complaints.

In this subchapter, we will explore the various stages of FMEA, including identification of failure modes, assessment of their severity, determination of their occurrence probability, and evaluation of detectability. We will also discuss the concept of Risk Priority Number (RPN), which is calculated by multiplying the severity, occurrence, and detectability scores. This number helps engineers prioritize failure modes for further analysis and action.

Furthermore, we will delve into the different types of FMEA, such as Design FMEA (DFMEA) and Process FMEA (PFMEA). DFMEA focuses on the identification and prevention of potential failure modes during the design phase, while PFMEA concentrates on failure modes associated with the manufacturing process itself.

Throughout this subchapter, we will provide real-life examples and case studies to illustrate the practical application of FMEA in the manufacturing engineering niche. By understanding and implementing FMEA effectively, engineers can minimize failures, improve product quality, and optimize manufacturing processes.

In conclusion, Failure Mode and Effects Analysis (FMEA) is a powerful tool for engineers in the field of manufacturing engineering. By proactively identifying potential failure modes and their effects, engineers can prevent failures, enhance product reliability, and optimize manufacturing processes. This subchapter will equip readers with the knowledge and skills required to implement FMEA successfully in their engineering endeavors.

Design of Experiments (DOE) in Troubleshooting

In the world of manufacturing engineering, troubleshooting is an inevitable part of the job. From identifying defects in products to resolving production bottlenecks, engineers are constantly challenged to find effective solutions. One powerful tool that can greatly enhance the troubleshooting process is the Design of Experiments (DOE) methodology.

DOE is a systematic approach that allows engineers to investigate the relationship between various factors and their impact on the outcome of a process. By conducting carefully designed experiments, engineers can gather valuable data, analyze it, and draw meaningful conclusions. This enables them to identify the root causes of problems and implement targeted solutions.

The key principle behind DOE is to vary multiple factors simultaneously, instead of changing them one at a time. This allows engineers to observe the interaction effects between different factors, which may not be evident when studying them individually. By considering all potential factors simultaneously, engineers can optimize the troubleshooting process and achieve more efficient and accurate results.

There are various types of DOE designs that engineers can utilize, depending on the complexity of the problem at hand. Some common designs include full factorial design, fractional factorial design, and response surface methodology. Each design has its own advantages and limitations, and engineers need to carefully select the appropriate one for their specific troubleshooting scenario.

DOE provides engineers with several benefits in the troubleshooting process. Firstly, it helps in reducing the number of experiments required to identify the root cause of a problem. By systematically varying multiple factors, engineers can quickly narrow down the potential causes and focus their efforts on the most influential ones.

Secondly, DOE enables engineers to quantify the impact of each factor on the process outcome. By analyzing the data collected from the experiments, engineers can determine the main effects and interaction effects of different factors. This information is crucial for making informed decisions and implementing effective solutions.

Lastly, DOE allows engineers to optimize the process parameters to achieve desired outcomes. By studying the relationship between factors and outcomes, engineers can identify the optimal settings for each factor to maximize the desired outcomes and minimize the occurrence of defects or issues.

In conclusion, Design of Experiments (DOE) is a powerful methodology that can greatly enhance the troubleshooting process in manufacturing engineering. By systematically varying multiple factors and analyzing the data collected, engineers can identify root causes, quantify the impact of factors, and optimize process parameters. Incorporating DOE into the troubleshooting toolkit can lead to more efficient and effective problem-solving, ultimately improving product quality and production efficiency.

Chapter 6: Case Studies in Troubleshooting

Case Study 1: Mechanical Failure in a Manufacturing Plant

Introduction:

In the world of manufacturing engineering, mechanical failures can be a significant challenge. These failures not only disrupt the production process but also result in financial losses and potential safety hazards. In this case study, we will explore a real-life example of a mechanical failure in a manufacturing plant and discuss the troubleshooting strategies employed to rectify the issue.

Background:

The manufacturing plant in question is a large-scale facility that produces automotive components. The plant operates around the clock, utilizing various machines and equipment to meet high production demands. One day, a critical machine suddenly malfunctioned, leading to a complete halt in production. The problem was identified as a mechanical failure, which required immediate attention to minimize downtime and losses.

Troubleshooting Process:

Upon discovering the mechanical failure, the plant's maintenance team quickly assembled to investigate and rectify the issue. The first step was to conduct a thorough inspection of the affected machine to identify the root cause of the problem. They discovered that a crucial component had failed, leading to the machine's inability to function properly.

After identifying the faulty component, the team procured a replacement part and began the repair process. However, they faced a challenge as the replacement part was a specialized component that was not readily available locally. In such a situation, the team resorted to contacting the equipment manufacturer directly, who promptly provided them with the required part.

With the replacement part in hand, the maintenance team proceeded with the repair, ensuring that all safety protocols were followed. Once the faulty component was replaced, the machine was thoroughly tested to ensure its proper functioning. After successful testing, the production process resumed, and the plant was back on track.

Conclusion:

This case study highlights the importance of troubleshooting strategies in the field of manufacturing engineering. Mechanical failures can occur unexpectedly, causing significant disruptions in production. In this instance, the maintenance team's swift response, effective problem identification, and collaboration with the equipment manufacturer played a crucial role in resolving the issue efficiently.

For manufacturing engineers and professionals, this case study serves as a reminder of the importance of proactive maintenance, regular inspections, and the need for contingency plans in case of mechanical failures. By learning from real-life examples, engineers can enhance their troubleshooting skills and develop strategies to mitigate potential risks, ensuring smooth operations and minimizing downtime in the manufacturing industry.

Case Study 2: Electrical System Malfunction in a Power Plant

Introduction:
Welcome to Case Study 2, where we explore a real-life scenario of an electrical system malfunction in a power plant. This case study aims to provide valuable insights and strategies for success in troubleshooting electrical issues, specifically within the manufacturing engineering niche.

Background:
Power plants are essential for generating electricity, and any malfunction in their electrical systems can have severe consequences. In this case, a power plant experienced a sudden blackout, leading to a complete shutdown of operations. The manufacturing engineers responsible for troubleshooting the issue faced immense pressure to identify and rectify the malfunction promptly.

Identifying the Problem:
The first step in troubleshooting is to identify the problem accurately. The engineers quickly realized that the blackout resulted from a fault in the electrical system. However, pinpointing the exact location of the fault proved challenging due to the complex network of cables, transformers, and generators involved.

Isolating the Fault:
To isolate the fault, the engineers employed various diagnostic techniques. They inspected the power distribution system, conducted detailed cable and connection checks, and utilized thermal imaging cameras to identify any overheating components. Additionally, they

analyzed historical data to identify any recent changes or anomalies in the system that could have triggered the malfunction.

Repair and Restoration:
Once the fault was isolated, the engineers devised a repair plan. They replaced damaged cables and faulty components, ensuring compliance with safety protocols. To avoid future malfunctions, they implemented preventive maintenance measures, such as regular inspections and equipment upgrades.

Lessons Learned:
This case study highlights several key lessons for manufacturing engineers:

1. Regular Maintenance: Power plants should have a robust maintenance schedule to identify and rectify potential issues before they escalate into major malfunctions.

2. Diagnostic Techniques: Utilizing advanced diagnostic tools, such as thermal imaging cameras, can significantly aid in identifying faults and reducing troubleshooting time.

3. Safety First: Engineers must always prioritize safety during troubleshooting activities, ensuring that proper safety protocols are followed to prevent accidents or injuries.

4. Documentation: Maintaining comprehensive documentation of the troubleshooting process, including the identified fault, repair procedures, and preventive measures, is crucial for future reference and continuous improvement.

Conclusion:

The electrical system malfunction in this power plant case study underscores the importance of efficient troubleshooting strategies in manufacturing engineering. By following a systematic approach to identify, isolate, repair, and prevent faults, engineers can minimize downtime, enhance safety, and optimize the performance of power plants.

Case Study 3: Software Bug in a Computer System

In the fast-paced world of manufacturing engineering, computer systems play a vital role in ensuring smooth operations and efficient production processes. However, even the most advanced systems can be susceptible to software bugs, which can lead to costly downtimes and disruptions in the manufacturing process. In this case study, we will explore a real-life example of a software bug in a computer system and the troubleshooting strategies employed to rectify the issue.

The Situation:
A manufacturing facility heavily relied on a computer system to control its assembly line, monitor inventory levels, and track production data. However, the system started experiencing intermittent failures, causing delays in production and leading to frustrated employees and customers. The manufacturing engineering team was tasked with identifying and resolving the issue promptly.

The Troubleshooting Process:
1. Gathering Information: The team began by collecting data related to the failures, such as error messages, timestamps, and affected modules. They also interviewed operators and technicians who had witnessed the failures firsthand to gain further insights.

2. Isolating the Issue: Using the collected data, the team identified patterns and narrowed down the problem to a specific module within the computer system. By isolating the issue, they could focus their troubleshooting efforts more effectively.

3. Analyzing the Code: The team delved into the software code of the module, meticulously examining each line for potential bugs. They

also reviewed any recent updates or modifications made to the system, considering the possibility of introducing new bugs inadvertently.

4. Testing and Validation: To verify their hypothesis, the team conducted rigorous testing, using simulated scenarios to recreate the failures. This step helped them confirm the presence of a software bug and pinpoint its exact location.

5. Bug Fixing: Armed with a thorough understanding of the bug, the team set out to develop a fix. They collaborated with software developers, ensuring that the solution addressed the root cause of the problem while minimizing any potential side effects.

6. Implementing the Fix: Once the fix was ready, the team carefully deployed it in a controlled environment. They closely monitored the system's performance, ensuring that the bug was indeed resolved without introducing new issues.

7. Preventive Measures: To prevent similar issues from occurring in the future, the manufacturing engineering team implemented robust quality assurance processes, including extensive testing protocols and regular code reviews.

By following these troubleshooting strategies, the manufacturing engineering team successfully resolved the software bug in the computer system, restoring smooth operations and minimizing production disruptions. This case study highlights the critical role of troubleshooting skills in the field of manufacturing engineering, emphasizing the importance of thorough analysis, effective collaboration, and preventive measures to ensure the longevity and reliability of computer systems in industrial settings.

Chapter 7: Preventive Measures and Continuous Improvement

Implementing Proactive Maintenance Strategies

In the ever-evolving field of manufacturing engineering, the importance of proactive maintenance strategies cannot be overstated. In order to ensure efficiency, productivity, and longevity of equipment and machinery, it is crucial to implement proactive maintenance measures. This subchapter will delve into the various strategies that can be employed to achieve this goal.

One of the key elements of proactive maintenance is regular equipment inspections. By conducting routine inspections, potential issues can be identified before they escalate into major problems. These inspections can include visual examinations, equipment performance evaluations, and thorough assessments of critical components. This proactive approach allows for early detection of defects, enabling timely repairs and preventing costly breakdowns.

Another effective strategy is the implementation of preventive maintenance schedules. This involves scheduling regular maintenance tasks such as lubrication, cleaning, and calibration to be performed at predetermined intervals. By adhering to a preventive maintenance schedule, manufacturing engineers can minimize the risk of unexpected breakdowns, optimize equipment performance, and extend the lifespan of machinery.

In addition, predictive maintenance techniques can be implemented to further enhance proactive maintenance strategies. By utilizing advanced technologies such as sensors and data analytics, manufacturing engineers can monitor the health and performance of equipment in real-time. This enables the detection of potential issues based on data patterns, allowing for timely intervention and minimizing downtime.

Furthermore, implementing condition-based maintenance can be a valuable strategy. By continuously monitoring the condition of equipment and analyzing the data collected, maintenance activities can be scheduled based on actual need rather than arbitrary time intervals. This approach maximizes the utilization of resources by focusing maintenance efforts where they are most needed, resulting in improved operational efficiency and reduced costs.

Lastly, fostering a culture of proactive maintenance within the organization is essential. This involves promoting awareness of the importance of maintenance, providing training to employees, and encouraging a proactive mindset. By emphasizing the significance of proactive maintenance, manufacturing engineers can instill a sense of responsibility and ownership among all stakeholders, ensuring the successful implementation of maintenance strategies.

In conclusion, implementing proactive maintenance strategies is crucial in the field of manufacturing engineering. By conducting regular inspections, adhering to preventive maintenance schedules, utilizing predictive and condition-based maintenance techniques, and fostering a culture of proactive maintenance, manufacturing engineers can optimize equipment performance, minimize downtime, and achieve long-term success in their operations.

Lessons Learned from Failure Analysis

Failure analysis is a critical aspect of troubleshooting and problem-solving in manufacturing engineering. It involves investigating and determining the root causes of failures in order to prevent their recurrence and improve overall performance and reliability. In this subchapter, we will explore the valuable lessons that can be gained from failure analysis and how they contribute to success in engineering.

One of the most important lessons learned from failure analysis is the necessity of a thorough and systematic approach to problem-solving. By carefully examining each component and process involved in a failure, engineers can identify the exact point of failure and the factors that contributed to it. This helps in developing effective solutions and implementing preventive measures to avoid similar failures in the future.

Another key lesson is the importance of data collection and analysis. Failure analysis relies heavily on accurate and detailed data, including failure rates, performance metrics, and environmental factors. By collecting and analyzing this data, engineers can gain insights into patterns and trends, allowing them to make informed decisions and optimize manufacturing processes.

Failure analysis also teaches engineers the significance of teamwork and collaboration. Successful failure analysis requires input from various disciplines, such as materials science, mechanical engineering, and quality control. By working together and combining their expertise, professionals can better understand the complex interactions that lead to failure and develop comprehensive solutions.

Furthermore, failure analysis highlights the value of continuous improvement. By constantly analyzing failures and implementing corrective actions, engineers can enhance product quality, reduce costs, and increase customer satisfaction. This iterative process of learning from failures and refining processes is essential for achieving long-term success in manufacturing engineering.

Finally, failure analysis teaches engineers the importance of a proactive mindset. Rather than reacting to failures as they occur, engineers should adopt a proactive approach by anticipating potential failure modes and implementing preventive measures. This mindset shift helps in identifying and addressing issues before they can impact the manufacturing process or the end product.

In conclusion, failure analysis is a powerful tool for learning and improvement in manufacturing engineering. By examining failures systematically, collecting and analyzing data, fostering collaboration, promoting continuous improvement, and adopting a proactive mindset, engineers can extract valuable lessons from failures. These lessons not only help in preventing future failures but also contribute to the overall success of engineering endeavors.

Continuous Improvement in Troubleshooting Processes

In the fast-paced world of manufacturing engineering, troubleshooting is an essential skill that can make or break the success of a project. Whether you are a seasoned engineer or just starting out in the field, it is crucial to understand the importance of continuously improving your troubleshooting processes.

Continuous improvement is not just a buzzword; it is a mindset that can transform the way you approach and solve problems. By constantly seeking ways to enhance your troubleshooting skills, you can become more efficient, effective, and ultimately, more successful in your role as a manufacturing engineer.

One of the key aspects of continuous improvement in troubleshooting processes is the need to embrace a proactive approach. Instead of waiting for problems to arise and then reacting to them, it is crucial to anticipate potential issues and develop strategies to mitigate them beforehand. This can be achieved through proper planning, thorough analysis, and the implementation of preventive measures. By doing so, you can minimize the occurrence of problems and improve the overall efficiency of your manufacturing processes.

Another important aspect of continuous improvement is the need to learn from every troubleshooting experience. Each problem you encounter is an opportunity to gain valuable insights and knowledge that can be applied to future situations. Take the time to analyze the root causes of the problem, identify any gaps in your knowledge or processes, and develop strategies to prevent similar issues from occurring in the future. By doing so, you can build a repository of best practices and lessons learned that will enable you to troubleshoot more effectively and efficiently in the long run.

Continuous improvement also involves staying updated with the latest advancements in technology and industry trends. Manufacturing engineering is a rapidly evolving field, and new tools, techniques, and methodologies are constantly being developed. By staying informed and embracing new technologies, you can enhance your troubleshooting capabilities and stay ahead of the curve.

In conclusion, continuous improvement in troubleshooting processes is essential for success in the field of manufacturing engineering. By adopting a proactive approach, learning from every experience, and staying updated with industry trends, you can enhance your skills, become more efficient, and ultimately achieve greater success as a manufacturing engineer. So, embrace the mindset of continuous improvement and watch your troubleshooting skills soar to new heights.

Chapter 8: Troubleshooting in Specific Engineering Disciplines

Mechanical Engineering Troubleshooting Strategies

Troubleshooting is an essential skill for every mechanical engineer, especially those in the field of manufacturing engineering. In the fast-paced and complex world of manufacturing, problems and challenges are bound to arise. Having effective troubleshooting strategies can make all the difference in ensuring successful outcomes and minimizing downtime. This subchapter aims to provide a comprehensive guide to mechanical engineering troubleshooting strategies, tailored specifically for professionals in the manufacturing engineering niche.

1. Define the Problem: The first step in troubleshooting is to clearly define the problem at hand. This involves gathering all available information, understanding the symptoms, and identifying the root cause. Utilize tools such as data analysis, observations, and interviews with relevant personnel to gain a comprehensive understanding of the issue.

2. Establish a Plan: Once the problem is defined, it's crucial to create a systematic plan of action. This plan should outline the steps to be taken, resources required, and an estimated timeline. Breaking down the problem into smaller, manageable tasks can help streamline the troubleshooting process.

3. Gather Expertise: In manufacturing engineering, collaboration is key. Seek input from experts in various fields to gain valuable insights

and alternative perspectives. This can include colleagues, suppliers, or even external consultants. Their expertise can prove invaluable in finding innovative solutions.

4. Utilize Troubleshooting Techniques: Mechanical engineers should be well-versed in various troubleshooting techniques. These include root cause analysis, fault tree analysis, fishbone diagrams, and failure mode and effects analysis (FMEA). Applying these techniques can help identify the underlying causes of the problem and develop effective solutions.

5. Test and Verify Solutions: After potential solutions are identified, it is essential to test and verify their effectiveness. Utilize simulations, prototypes, or small-scale trials to assess the feasibility and performance of proposed solutions. This iterative process allows for adjustments and optimizations.

6. Document and Communicate: Throughout the troubleshooting process, maintain detailed documentation of the steps taken, results obtained, and solutions implemented. This documentation serves as a valuable resource for future reference and can aid in preventing similar issues from recurring. Effective communication with stakeholders is also crucial, ensuring everyone is informed of progress and potential impacts.

By following these mechanical engineering troubleshooting strategies, manufacturing engineers can enhance their problem-solving skills, minimize downtime, and improve overall productivity. Troubleshooting is an art that requires a combination of technical knowledge, analytical thinking, and effective communication. With practice and experience, engineers can master this art and become invaluable assets to their organizations.

Electrical Engineering Troubleshooting Strategies

In the fast-paced world of manufacturing engineering, electrical issues can arise at any moment, causing delays in production and costing companies valuable time and resources. This subchapter, "Electrical Engineering Troubleshooting Strategies," aims to equip individuals with the knowledge and strategies needed to effectively address and resolve electrical problems in a manufacturing setting.

Electrical troubleshooting requires a systematic approach to identify and fix faults in electrical systems. By following a step-by-step process, engineers can minimize downtime and keep operations running smoothly. This subchapter will outline the key strategies that can be employed to tackle electrical issues effectively.

The first strategy is to gather as much information as possible about the problem at hand. This involves understanding the symptoms, collecting data, and consulting relevant documentation. By having a clear understanding of the issue, engineers can narrow down the potential causes and devise a plan of action.

Next, it is crucial to perform a thorough inspection of the electrical system. This includes checking for loose connections, damaged cables, or faulty components. By visually inspecting the system, engineers can often identify obvious faults and eliminate them as potential causes.

Once the initial inspection is complete, engineers can move on to more advanced troubleshooting techniques, such as using test equipment to measure voltages, currents, and resistances. This allows for a more detailed analysis of the electrical system and can help pinpoint the root cause of the problem.

Additionally, this subchapter will delve into common electrical issues encountered in manufacturing engineering, such as motor failures, circuit overloads, and electrical noise. Each issue will be explored in detail, with specific troubleshooting strategies provided.

Lastly, this subchapter will emphasize the importance of safety when troubleshooting electrical systems. Electrical hazards can pose significant risks, so it is crucial to follow safety protocols, use personal protective equipment, and work with a qualified team.

In conclusion, "Electrical Engineering Troubleshooting Strategies" offers a comprehensive guide to troubleshooting electrical issues in a manufacturing engineering setting. By following the outlined strategies, individuals can efficiently diagnose and resolve electrical problems, minimizing downtime and maximizing productivity. Whether you are an experienced engineer or new to the field, this subchapter provides valuable insights and techniques for success in electrical troubleshooting.

Civil Engineering Troubleshooting Strategies

In the field of civil engineering, troubleshooting is an essential skill that engineers need to possess in order to ensure the successful completion of construction projects. From designing and building structures to managing complex infrastructure systems, civil engineers face numerous challenges that require quick thinking and effective problem-solving abilities. This subchapter aims to provide valuable insights and strategies on troubleshooting in civil engineering, helping engineers overcome common issues encountered in the manufacturing engineering niche.

One of the key aspects of troubleshooting in civil engineering is identifying the root cause of problems. Whether it's a structural failure, material deficiency, or construction error, understanding the underlying issues is crucial to implementing the most appropriate solutions. This subchapter will delve into the different techniques and approaches that engineers can utilize to pinpoint the causes of problems accurately.

Furthermore, the content will also highlight the importance of effective communication and collaboration in troubleshooting. Civil engineering projects often involve multidisciplinary teams, including architects, contractors, and various specialists. The ability to communicate effectively with team members, stakeholders, and clients is essential for successful troubleshooting. This subchapter will provide valuable tips on improving communication skills and fostering collaboration among diverse professionals within the manufacturing engineering niche.

Moreover, the content will explore specific troubleshooting strategies applicable to manufacturing engineering in civil engineering projects. It will cover topics such as quality control, risk management, and cost optimization. These strategies aim to address common challenges faced in manufacturing processes, such as material selection, fabrication, and assembly. By providing practical examples and case studies, this subchapter will equip engineers with the necessary tools and knowledge to troubleshoot manufacturing-related issues effectively.

Lastly, this subchapter will emphasize the importance of continuous learning and staying updated with the latest advancements in civil engineering. With technology evolving rapidly, engineers need to keep up with new methodologies, materials, and software tools. The content will provide resources and recommendations to help engineers stay informed and enhance their troubleshooting skills in the manufacturing engineering niche.

In conclusion, the subchapter "Civil Engineering Troubleshooting Strategies" aims to provide engineers in the manufacturing engineering niche with valuable insights and strategies to overcome common challenges in civil engineering projects. By focusing on root cause analysis, effective communication, and specific troubleshooting techniques, this content will empower engineers to tackle manufacturing-related issues successfully. Additionally, it will emphasize the need for continuous learning and staying updated with the latest advancements in civil engineering to ensure long-term success in the field.

Software Engineering Troubleshooting Strategies

In today's fast-paced technological world, software engineering plays a crucial role in various industries, including manufacturing engineering. However, even the most well-designed software can encounter issues or bugs that hinder its performance. That's where troubleshooting strategies come into play. In this subchapter, we will explore effective methods and approaches to identify, analyze, and resolve software-related problems, specifically tailored to the manufacturing engineering niche.

1. Understanding the Problem: The first step in troubleshooting any software issue is to gain a deep understanding of the problem at hand. This involves gathering detailed information about the symptoms, error messages, and the context in which the problem occurs. By analyzing this data, engineers can narrow down the potential causes and focus their efforts on finding an appropriate solution.

2. Reproducing the Problem: Reproducing the problem is essential in troubleshooting software issues. Engineers should attempt to recreate the problem in a controlled environment, which helps in isolating the root cause. This process may involve replicating the inputs, configurations, or scenarios that trigger the problem. By successfully reproducing the problem, engineers can perform more accurate diagnostics and validate potential solutions.

3. Analyzing the Code: In software engineering troubleshooting, analyzing the code is vital to identify any coding errors or logical flaws that may be causing the problem. This requires a careful examination of the codebase, including the affected modules, functions, and

variables. Engineers should leverage debugging tools, log files, and code review techniques to identify any potential issues and their impact on the software's behavior.

4. Collaborative Problem Solving: Troubleshooting software issues is often a collaborative effort. Engineers should actively communicate and collaborate with colleagues, stakeholders, and even software vendors to gather insights, share knowledge, and brainstorm potential solutions. Collaborative problem-solving not only enhances the chances of finding effective solutions but also fosters a culture of continuous improvement within the manufacturing engineering industry.

5. Documentation and Knowledge Sharing: Throughout the troubleshooting process, it is crucial to document all steps taken, including the identified problems, potential solutions, and their outcomes. This documentation serves as a valuable resource for future reference and helps in building a knowledge base within the organization. Sharing this knowledge with other software engineers and stakeholders promotes learning and enables faster troubleshooting in the future.

In conclusion, software engineering troubleshooting strategies are indispensable in the manufacturing engineering niche. By following a systematic approach, understanding the problem, analyzing the code, collaborating with others, and documenting the process, engineers can effectively identify and resolve software-related issues. These strategies not only ensure the smooth functioning of software systems but also contribute to continuous improvement and innovation within the manufacturing industry as a whole.

Chapter 9: Troubleshooting Challenges in Emerging Technologies

Troubleshooting in Renewable Energy Systems

Renewable energy systems have emerged as a vital component in the quest for sustainable and eco-friendly power generation. With their increasing popularity and widespread adoption, it is crucial to have a comprehensive understanding of troubleshooting techniques specific to these systems. This subchapter aims to equip individuals, particularly those in the manufacturing engineering niche, with the knowledge and skills required to effectively troubleshoot renewable energy systems.

1. Introduction to Renewable Energy Systems: To lay the foundation for troubleshooting, this section provides a brief overview of various renewable energy systems, including solar, wind, hydro, geothermal, and biomass. Understanding the fundamental principles and components of these systems is essential before diving into troubleshooting techniques.

2. Common Issues in Renewable Energy Systems: This section highlights the typical problems encountered in renewable energy systems, such as equipment malfunctions, electrical or mechanical failures, environmental factors, and system integration issues. By identifying these common issues, individuals can develop a systematic approach to troubleshooting.

3. Troubleshooting Methodology: Here, we outline a step-by-step methodology for effective

troubleshooting in renewable energy systems. This includes initial assessment, gathering information, isolating the problem, formulating hypotheses, testing and verifying hypotheses, and implementing solutions. Real-life case studies and examples specific to manufacturing engineering will be provided to enhance understanding.

4. Tools and Equipment for Troubleshooting: This section focuses on the tools and equipment necessary for troubleshooting renewable energy systems. It covers basic tools, such as multimeters, clamp meters, and infrared cameras, as well as specialized equipment like power quality analyzers and data loggers. Additionally, guidance on their proper usage and interpretation of results will be provided.

5. Preventive Maintenance and Best Practices: To minimize the occurrence of problems in renewable energy systems, this section emphasizes the importance of preventive maintenance. It covers regular inspections, cleaning, lubrication, calibration, and replacement of components. Best practices for ensuring optimal system performance and longevity will also be discussed.

6. Troubleshooting Safety: Safety should always be a top priority when troubleshooting renewable energy systems. This section addresses potential hazards and safety precautions specific to these systems. It includes guidelines for working at heights, handling electrical components, and dealing with hazardous materials.

By delving into the intricacies of troubleshooting in renewable energy systems, this subchapter aims to empower individuals in the manufacturing engineering niche to overcome challenges and ensure optimal performance of these sustainable energy sources. Whether you are a technician, engineer, or an enthusiast, this valuable resource will equip you with the knowledge and skills necessary to effectively troubleshoot renewable energy systems and contribute to a greener future.

Troubleshooting in Internet of Things (IoT) Devices

In today's rapidly evolving world, the Internet of Things (IoT) has become an integral part of our daily lives, revolutionizing the way we interact with technology. From smart homes to industrial automation, IoT devices have opened up endless possibilities for innovation and convenience. However, like any technology, IoT devices are not immune to malfunctions and issues that can disrupt their smooth functioning. In this subchapter, we will explore common troubleshooting strategies for IoT devices, specifically addressing the audience of manufacturing engineering professionals.

One of the first steps in troubleshooting IoT devices is to identify the possible causes of the problem. This may involve examining the hardware, software, network connectivity, or even user error. Manufacturing engineers should be well-versed in the specific IoT devices they are working with, understanding their architecture, functionality, and potential limitations. This knowledge will prove invaluable when diagnosing and resolving issues.

Once the cause of the problem has been identified, it is crucial to isolate and narrow down the scope of the issue. This can involve checking the physical connections, ensuring proper power supply, or verifying the integrity of the network. In manufacturing engineering, where IoT devices are often employed for process automation and data collection, issues related to sensors, actuators, or data transmission may arise. Troubleshooting may require inspecting these components and verifying their proper functioning.

Another essential aspect of troubleshooting IoT devices is understanding the software and firmware that operate them. Updates and patches can address known bugs and vulnerabilities, so it is vital to keep IoT devices up to date with the latest software versions. Additionally, firmware compatibility issues may arise when integrating multiple IoT devices within a manufacturing environment. Ensuring that all devices are running compatible firmware versions can help prevent compatibility-related problems.

Furthermore, the network infrastructure supporting IoT devices should be assessed when troubleshooting. Issues related to poor signal strength, interference, or network congestion can significantly impact the performance of IoT devices. Conducting a thorough analysis of the network and addressing any bottlenecks or shortcomings will help ensure the smooth operation of the IoT ecosystem.

In conclusion, troubleshooting IoT devices requires a comprehensive understanding of their architecture, functionality, and potential issues. Manufacturing engineering professionals should possess the knowledge and skills necessary to diagnose and resolve problems related to hardware, software, network connectivity, and user error. By following the strategies outlined in this subchapter, engineers can minimize downtime, maximize efficiency, and ensure the successful integration of IoT devices within manufacturing processes.

Troubleshooting in Artificial Intelligence Systems

Artificial Intelligence (AI) systems have become an integral part of various industries, including manufacturing engineering. These systems help streamline processes, enhance productivity, and improve overall efficiency. However, like any complex technology, AI systems can encounter issues that require troubleshooting. In this subchapter, we will explore some common troubleshooting strategies for AI systems, specifically in the context of manufacturing engineering.

One of the most critical aspects of troubleshooting AI systems is understanding the underlying algorithms and models. Manufacturing engineers need to have a solid grasp of the AI system's architecture, data inputs, and expected outputs. By thoroughly understanding the inner workings of the AI system, engineers can identify potential bottlenecks and pinpoint areas that may cause problems.

Data quality is another crucial consideration in troubleshooting AI systems. Garbage in, garbage out – the saying holds true for AI systems as well. If the input data is flawed or lacks relevance, the AI system's performance will suffer. Engineers should carefully analyze the data sources, assess data quality, and ensure that the data used for training the AI system is representative of real-world scenarios. Regular data audits and updates are also essential to maintain the AI system's accuracy.

When troubleshooting AI systems, engineers should also pay attention to the system's output and feedback loops. Monitoring the system's performance and analyzing the results it produces can help identify anomalies or errors. Feedback loops allow engineers to gather insights from end-users and stakeholders, providing valuable information for troubleshooting. Regularly seeking feedback and conducting user acceptance testing can help identify and resolve issues promptly.

Collaboration and knowledge sharing are vital components of successful troubleshooting in AI systems. Engineers should actively engage with other professionals in the field, share experiences, and learn from each other's successes and challenges. Online communities, forums, and professional networks can serve as valuable resources for troubleshooting AI systems.

Finally, documenting troubleshooting processes and solutions is crucial for future reference and continuous improvement. By maintaining a knowledge base of troubleshooting strategies and their outcomes, engineers can save time and effort in resolving similar issues in the future.

In conclusion, troubleshooting AI systems in manufacturing engineering requires a comprehensive understanding of the system's architecture, data quality, and feedback loops. Regular monitoring, collaboration, and documentation are essential for addressing issues promptly and improving the overall performance of AI systems. By employing these strategies, manufacturing engineers can ensure the smooth operation of AI systems and unlock their full potential in enhancing productivity and efficiency in the manufacturing industry.

Chapter 10: Professional Development for Troubleshooters

Continuous Learning in Troubleshooting

In the fast-paced world of manufacturing engineering, troubleshooting skills are essential for success. Whether you are a seasoned professional or just starting out in the field, the ability to effectively identify and solve problems is crucial. However, troubleshooting is not a static skill that can be learned once and applied forever. It requires continuous learning and adaptation in order to keep up with evolving technologies and complex systems.

Continuous learning in troubleshooting is about staying curious, open-minded, and willing to explore new ideas and approaches. It is about embracing a growth mindset and recognizing that there is always room for improvement. By committing to ongoing learning, you can enhance your problem-solving abilities and become a more valuable asset to your organization.

One way to foster continuous learning in troubleshooting is to actively seek out new knowledge and information. Stay updated on the latest advancements in manufacturing engineering through industry publications, conferences, and online forums. Engage with experts in the field and learn from their experiences. By staying informed, you can expand your technical knowledge and gain insights into emerging trends and best practices.

Another important aspect of continuous learning in troubleshooting is reflection and analysis. After resolving a problem, take the time to reflect on the process and evaluate your approach. What worked well? What could have been done differently? By critically analyzing your troubleshooting methods, you can identify areas for improvement and refine your problem-solving techniques.

Additionally, learning from past experiences and mistakes is a valuable part of continuous learning in troubleshooting. Keep a record of the problems you have encountered and the solutions you have implemented. Review these records periodically to identify patterns or recurring issues. By understanding the root causes of problems, you can develop strategies to prevent them from occurring in the future.

Collaboration and knowledge sharing are also essential for continuous learning in troubleshooting. Engage with colleagues and experts in your field to exchange ideas, discuss challenges, and learn from each other's experiences. Participate in brainstorming sessions and problem-solving workshops to gain new perspectives and approaches.

In conclusion, continuous learning in troubleshooting is a vital skill for manufacturing engineers. By staying curious, seeking out new knowledge, reflecting on past experiences, and collaborating with others, you can enhance your problem-solving abilities and stay ahead in the ever-evolving field of manufacturing engineering. Embrace continuous learning as a lifelong journey and watch your troubleshooting skills thrive.

Certifications and Training for Troubleshooters

In the highly competitive field of manufacturing engineering, it is essential for professionals to possess the necessary skills and knowledge to troubleshoot and resolve issues effectively. Troubleshooting is an art that requires a unique set of problem-solving abilities, technical expertise, and a deep understanding of the manufacturing process. To succeed in this demanding field, individuals must invest in certifications and training programs that enhance their troubleshooting capabilities.

Certifications play a vital role in validating a troubleshooter's competence and expertise. They provide tangible evidence of a professional's skills and knowledge, making them highly sought after by employers. One such certification widely recognized in the manufacturing engineering industry is the Certified Manufacturing Troubleshooter (CMT) credential. Offered by esteemed organizations, the CMT certification confirms that an individual possesses the necessary skills to diagnose and resolve complex manufacturing issues efficiently. This certification addresses various aspects of troubleshooting, including fault identification, root cause analysis, and effective problem-solving techniques.

While certifications are crucial, ongoing training is equally important for troubleshooters to stay ahead in their field. Training programs offer the opportunity to acquire new skills, update existing knowledge, and learn about the latest technological advancements. These programs can be industry-specific, focusing on areas such as machinery troubleshooting, process optimization, or quality control. Additionally, training courses in communication and leadership skills can greatly enhance a troubleshooter's ability to collaborate with cross-functional teams, effectively communicate findings, and lead problem-solving initiatives.

To ensure comprehensive training, troubleshooters should seek out a combination of classroom-based instruction, hands-on experience, and interactive workshops. This multifaceted approach allows individuals to apply theoretical knowledge to real-world scenarios, developing their troubleshooting skills in a practical setting. Training programs that offer case studies and simulations further enhance the learning experience, enabling troubleshooters to tackle complex problems without real-world consequences.

In conclusion, certifications and training programs are essential components of a successful career in manufacturing engineering. They provide troubleshooters with the necessary skills, knowledge, and credentials to effectively diagnose and resolve complex issues. By investing in certifications such as the CMT and participating in ongoing training, professionals can continuously enhance their troubleshooting abilities, positioning themselves as valuable assets in the manufacturing industry. Whether you are an aspiring troubleshooter or an experienced professional, certifications and training programs are a crucial stepping stone to success in this challenging field.

Networking and Knowledge Sharing Opportunities

In today's fast-paced world of manufacturing engineering, it is crucial to stay updated with the latest trends, technologies, and best practices. One of the most effective ways to do so is by actively engaging in networking and knowledge sharing opportunities. By connecting with peers, experts, and industry leaders, you can gain valuable insights, expand your professional network, and enhance your troubleshooting skills.

Networking events, conferences, and seminars provide a unique platform for professionals in manufacturing engineering to come together, exchange ideas, and learn from each other's experiences. These events bring together individuals from various backgrounds, including engineers, managers, researchers, and entrepreneurs. By attending such gatherings, you not only get the chance to meet like-minded individuals but also have the opportunity to build lasting relationships that can help you throughout your career.

Participating in networking events also allows you to stay informed about the latest industry trends and technological advancements. By engaging in discussions, asking questions, and attending workshops, you can gain insights into emerging technologies, innovative manufacturing processes, and cutting-edge research. This knowledge can be invaluable in troubleshooting complex engineering problems and finding innovative solutions.

Additionally, networking events often feature keynote speakers who are experts in their fields. These industry leaders share their experiences, success stories, and lessons learned, providing you with a unique perspective on troubleshooting strategies. By carefully listening to their advice and incorporating their insights into your own problem-solving approach, you can accelerate your professional growth and become a more effective troubleshooter.

Apart from physical networking events, the digital era has opened up a world of virtual networking opportunities. Online forums, discussion groups, and social media platforms provide avenues for professionals in manufacturing engineering to connect with each other, regardless of geographical boundaries. These platforms enable you to ask questions, seek advice, and share your knowledge with a wider audience, thereby expanding your reach and fostering collaborations.

In conclusion, networking and knowledge sharing opportunities are essential for success in the field of manufacturing engineering. By actively participating in networking events, conferences, online forums, and social media groups, you can build a strong professional network, stay updated with the latest industry trends, and gain valuable insights from experts. Embracing these opportunities will not only enhance your troubleshooting skills but also contribute to your overall professional growth.

Chapter 11: Conclusion and Final Thoughts

Recap of Key Strategies for Successful Troubleshooting

In the fast-paced world of manufacturing engineering, troubleshooting is an essential skill that can make or break the success of a project. Whether you're a seasoned professional or just starting out in the field, having a solid understanding of the key strategies for successful troubleshooting is crucial. In this subchapter, we will recap the most important strategies that can help you overcome any challenge that comes your way.

First and foremost, it's essential to approach troubleshooting with a systematic mindset. This means breaking down the problem into smaller, more manageable parts and analyzing each component individually. By doing so, you can identify the root cause of the issue and develop a targeted solution. Remember, troubleshooting is not about guesswork; it's about collecting data, analyzing it, and making informed decisions.

Another critical strategy is to maintain a clear and open line of communication with your team members and stakeholders. Collaboration is key in troubleshooting, as it allows for a diversity of perspectives and expertise to be brought to the table. By fostering an environment where everyone can freely share their thoughts and ideas, you'll be able to tackle problems from multiple angles and find innovative solutions.

Additionally, keeping detailed records throughout the troubleshooting process is paramount. Documenting every step you take, including the observations, tests performed, and solutions attempted, will not only help you stay organized but also serve as a valuable resource for future reference. By maintaining a comprehensive troubleshooting log, you can build upon your past experiences and avoid repeating mistakes.

Furthermore, it's crucial to stay up-to-date with the latest technologies and industry trends. The field of manufacturing engineering is constantly evolving, and new tools and techniques are being developed every day. By staying informed and continuously expanding your knowledge base, you'll be better equipped to troubleshoot modern systems and resolve complex issues.

Lastly, never underestimate the power of continuous learning and professional development. Troubleshooting is a skill that can always be honed and improved upon. Seek out opportunities to attend workshops, conferences, and training sessions to further enhance your troubleshooting abilities. Additionally, don't be afraid to learn from your mistakes and seek feedback from your colleagues. Embrace a growth mindset and never stop striving for excellence.

In conclusion, successful troubleshooting in manufacturing engineering requires a systematic approach, effective communication, meticulous record-keeping, staying current with industry trends, and a commitment to continuous learning. By incorporating these key strategies into your troubleshooting toolkit, you'll be well-equipped to overcome any challenge that comes your way and achieve success in your engineering endeavors.

The Future of Troubleshooting in Engineering

The future of troubleshooting in engineering holds immense potential and exciting possibilities for the field of manufacturing engineering. As technology advances and becomes more complex, the need for efficient and effective troubleshooting methods becomes crucial. This subchapter aims to explore the emerging trends and strategies that will shape the future of troubleshooting in engineering, with a specific focus on the manufacturing engineering niche.

One prominent trend that will revolutionize troubleshooting is the integration of artificial intelligence (AI) and machine learning (ML) algorithms. By leveraging the power of AI and ML, engineers will be able to develop smart systems that can autonomously identify and resolve issues in real-time. These intelligent systems will not only enhance the efficiency of troubleshooting but also minimize downtime and improve overall productivity in manufacturing processes. The ability to predict and prevent potential failures will significantly reduce costs and enhance the quality of products.

Furthermore, the future of troubleshooting will witness the rise of remote diagnostics and troubleshooting capabilities. With advancements in connectivity and the Internet of Things (IoT), engineers will be able to remotely monitor and troubleshoot equipment and processes. This will eliminate the need for physical presence on-site, saving time and resources while providing instant solutions. Remote troubleshooting will also facilitate collaboration between engineers, enabling them to share expertise and resolve complex issues collectively.

Another key aspect of the future of troubleshooting in engineering is the utilization of data analytics and visualization techniques. With the increasing availability of big data, engineers can analyze vast amounts of information to identify patterns, trends, and root causes of problems. Visualizing data through interactive dashboards and graphs will enable engineers to gain valuable insights and make informed decisions. This data-driven approach will empower engineers to troubleshoot proactively, rather than reactively, by addressing potential issues before they lead to critical failures.

Moreover, the future of troubleshooting will embrace augmented reality (AR) and virtual reality (VR) technologies. These immersive technologies will provide engineers with virtual environments to simulate and troubleshoot complex systems. AR overlays can guide engineers with step-by-step instructions, while VR can offer a realistic representation of the equipment or process. By enabling engineers to visually explore and interact with virtual models, AR and VR will enhance troubleshooting accuracy and speed.

In conclusion, the future of troubleshooting in engineering, particularly in the manufacturing engineering niche, is set to be transformed by the integration of AI and ML, remote diagnostics, data analytics, and AR/VR technologies. These advancements will revolutionize the way engineers identify and resolve issues, leading to improved efficiency, reduced downtime, and enhanced productivity. Embracing these emerging trends and strategies will be crucial for engineers to stay ahead in the rapidly evolving field of troubleshooting.

www.ingramcontent.com/pod-product-compliance
Lightning Source LLC
LaVergne TN
LVHW052000060526
838201LV00059B/3754